ACQUIRING AND USING POTIONS AND CONSUMABLES IN *FORTNITE*®

JESSICA SHAW

Enslow Publishing
101 W. 23rd Street
Suite 240
New York, NY 10011
USA
enslow.com

Published in 2020 by Enslow Publishing, LLC
101 W. 23rd Street, Suite 240, New York, NY 10011

Library of Congress Cataloging-in-Publication Data

Names: Shaw, Jessica.
Title: Acquiring and using potions and consumables in Fortnite® / Jessica Shaw.
Description: New York : Enslow Publishing, 2020. | Series: The unofficial
Fortnite® survival guide | Includes glossary and index.
Identifiers: ISBN 9781978517035 (pbk.) | ISBN 9781978517059
(library bound) | ISBN 9781978517042 (6 pack)
Subjects: LCSH: Fortnite Battle Royale (Game)--Juvenile literature. | Imaginary
wars and battles--Juvenile literature. | Video games--Juvenile literature.
Classification: LCC GV1469.35.F67 S57 2020 | DDC 794.8--dc23

Fortnite is a trademark of Epic Games, and its use in this book does not
imply a recommendation or endorsement of this title by Epic Games.

Printed in the United States of America

To Our Readers: We have done our best to make sure all website addresses in this book
were active and appropriate when we went to press. However, the author and the publisher
have no control over and assume no liability for the material available on those websites
or on any websites they may link to. Any comments or suggestions can be sent by email to
customerservice@enslow.com.

CONTENTS

INTRODUCTION

On October 12, 1958, a long line formed in front of a small computer in Brookhaven, New York. It was Visitors' Day at Brookhaven National Laboratory, and everyone was waiting for a chance to try out what would become known as the first video game. Hoping to prove to visitors that the work done at the laboratory was both interesting and important, a physicist named William Higinbotham had invented a simple game of tennis that could be played on the analog computer. The game was called *Tennis for Two*. The small screen showed only a line for the ground, one for the net, and a small dot that represented the tennis ball. Players turned a knob to adjust the angle of the ball and pushed a button to hit the ball. As simple as it was, no one had ever seen anything like it, and visitors loved it!

In the many decades since Higinbotham's invention, thousands of video games have been created. Many of them became very popular, but with more than two hundred million active players and earnings of more than $1 billion in its first year, some say *Fortnite*, launched in

Tennis for Two, a simple game invented in 1958, marked the beginning of the multibillion-dollar video game industry.

2017 by Epic Games, may go down in history as the most successful video game ever. The amazing success of *Fortnite* can be attributed to a unique combination of elements. *Fortnite* can be played on numerous different platforms: PC, Mac, PlayStation 4, Xbox One, Nintendo Switch, Apple iPhones and iPads, and many Android devices. While most video games must be purchased, the most popular mode of *Fortnite*, Battle Royale, is free. It's played in real time, with each match between up to one hundred new competitors. Players can customize their soldier and enjoy the challenges of ever-changing elements in the game. Frequent updates and additions to the weapons and loot items are available. Among the most popular loot items are the powerful potions and consumables—no soldier can survive on *Fortnite's* epic online battlefield without them!

CHAPTER 1

Slurping for Survival: Potions and Consumables

In a typical *Fortnite*: Battle Royale match, there are up to one hundred players competing on an island, each hoping to have the last soldier standing. To win, a player needs to have the experience and skills necessary to defeat other players while surviving dangerous conditions on the island. There are a variety of weapons, tools, and building resources to use in the game, but some of the most valuable items are the potions and consumables that keep soldiers alive.

What Is a Consumable?

Fortnite consumables are goods called Powerup Loot items. They are one-time use items, which means that they disappear after use or wear

Drinking one of the potions found on the *Fortnite* battlefield is a popular way to boost a soldier's Health or Shield.

off eventually. The amount of time it takes to use a consumable varies from item to item. Players are vulnerable to attacks while they are waiting for a consumable to take effect, so it's important to use them while in a safe location, if possible.

Purpose of Consumables

Soldiers in the game must have both Health and Shields. At the beginning of a match, each soldier's Health meter is at one hundred.

TYLER BLEVINS: *FORTNITE* GAMER EXTRAORDINAIRE

In a game as challenging as *Fortnite*, many players are thrilled to win even one match. After all, winning a match means defeating up to ninety-nine other players! But for the gamer known as Ninja, one win was only the beginning. Ninja is Tyler Blevins, the first professional video

Tyler Blevins is a professional gamer who makes a living doing what he loves by playing *Fortnite* for up to twelve hours every day!

game player to have his picture on the front of *ESPN The Magazine*. He plays for around twelve hours each day and makes a living streaming his *Fortnite* matches online to his more than ten million followers. So how much does a world-famous gamer make for playing *Fortnite* every day? Blevins's income is estimated to be a whopping $500,000 a month!

9

Food consumables are another way to power up during a *Fortnite* battle.

The Shield meter starts at zero and must be activated by using the right consumables. Some consumables restore Health, some activate and boost Shields, and some can do both.

Types of Consumables

There are many different consumables in *Fortnite*. Two of them are potions that soldiers can drink, a Shield Potion and a Small Shield Potion. There are two other drinkable consumables, a Chug Jug and Slurp Juice. Apples and Mushrooms are two of the food consumables. Med Kits and Bandages are medical supply consumables, and the Bush is a consumable that is worn as a disguise.

CHAPTER 2

Shield Boosting with Powerup Loot

W hen beginning a match, players will need to "power up" with special loot that can activate their Shields. As the game goes on, players will need to continuously replenish their Shields as they are depleted. There are several types of Powerup Loot that can boost Shields.

Shield Potion

The Shield Potion is considered rare but is not too difficult to find. It can be found in Supply Drops and inside Supply Llamas and Chests. It can sometimes be purchased in Rare Vending Machines. Shield Potions take five seconds to use and replenish a soldier's Shield meter by fifty points. The Shield Potion can't protect

In order to survive a *Fortnite* battle, a soldier's Shield meter must not be depleted.

against damage from falls or the Storm on the island.

Small Shield Potion

The Small Shield Potion is rated as uncommon. It is found inside Chests or anywhere out in the wild. This potion is convenient because it takes only two seconds to use. It boosts a soldier's Shield meter by twenty-five points. However, like the Shield Potion, the Small Shield Potion

13

THREE WAYS TO PLAY: *FORTNITE* GAME MODES

The most popular mode of play in *Fortnite* is *Fortnite*: Battle Royale. In *Fortnite*: **Battle Royale**, one hundred players are dropped onto the island to battle each other. Within Battle Royale, there are several different options. Players can choose solo, duos, squads, or a 50 versus 50 match. For players wanting to join forces, duo matches consist of two-player teams, squads means players can

Players can choose from several different game modes in *Fortnite* and can play solo or team up with friends.

work in four-player teams, and 50 versus 50 matches divide the players into two teams. Another mode is the Creative mode, in which players can practice skills and explore without being killed. Lastly, there is a player versus environment (PvE) mode called *Fortnite*: Save the World. In this fun mode, up to four players can join forces to complete missions and defeat the zombie-like creatures that have taken over the world!

can't protect against falls or the Storm. Also, this potion can boost Shields only up to fifty points, so soldiers with Shield meters at fifty or above can't use it.

Mushrooms

Mushrooms are found in swampy areas and shaded, woody areas in the wild. They work within one second and boost Shields by five points. Unfortunately, Mushrooms can't be stored and carried. They must be consumed when they're found, so if a soldier's Shield meter is already at 100 points when a Mushroom is found, it can't be used.

CHAPTER 3

Essential Items for Soldier Health

A soldier's Health can be depleted by injuries from falls, fights, or the Storm. If a soldier's Health meter reaches zero, they are eliminated. Throughout the match, soldiers will need to replenish their Health with special Health-boosting consumables.

Bandages

Bandages are a common, easily found item. They are dropped in stacks of five and can be found in Chests, Supply Llamas, Supply Drops, Floor Loot, and Vending Machines. They take four seconds to use, and they boost a soldier's Health meter by fifteen points. One drawback of bandages is that they can boost a Health meter only up to seventy-five points, so soldiers

Injuries are part of the game, so it's important to know about the different *Fortnite* consumables that will boost an injured soldier's Health.

above that level will need to use a different consumable to boost their Health.

Med Kits

Med Kits are powerful healing consumables. They are uncommon and not as easy to find as Bandages but can be found in Chests, Supply Drops, Supply Llamas, Floor Loot, and Vending Machines. Med Kits restore a soldier's Health meter back to one hundred.

HOW TO SURVIVE THE STORM

As if it's not enough of a challenge for a player to stay alive in a match against ninety-nine others, in a *Fortnite*: Battle Royale match, soldiers must also survive the deadly Storm! Each player's map will have the safe zone marked with a circle. If a player is able to keep his or her soldier within that circle, damage from the Storm can be avoided. When caught outside of that safe area, the blue line on the map shows players the shortest route to safety. Soldiers low on Health will need to replenish their Health quickly and reach safety. Bandages can be used to quickly restore fifteen points of Health, at which point the soldier can take off running toward the safe zone. If a soldier's Health needs a bigger boost, a Med Kit is worth its weight in gold!

YOU ARE IN THE STORM. Run!

To stay in the game, players must know where to find essential consumables to keep up their soldiers' Health and Shield meters.

Players need to get their soldiers to the safe zone as quickly as possible when the deadly *Fortnite* Storm hits.

They take ten seconds to use, so soldiers need to be in a safe place when using this valuable healing consumable.

Apples

Like Mushrooms, Apples are easy to find. They are out in the wild, under and around trees. They work almost instantly and increase a soldier's Health meter by five points. They can't be stored and carried, so must be used when and where they are found.

CHAPTER 4

Playing to Win: Other Powerful Consumables

Some of the most powerful and useful consumables are needed if a player is to survive very long in a match. As the Storm closes in and opponents are drawn closer together near the end of the match, players will want to be prepared by having essential consumables in their backpacks.

Slurp Juice

Slurp Juice is an Epic consumable, meaning it is valuable and difficult to find. It takes only two seconds to consume Slurp Juice. It restores a soldier's Health at the rate of one point every half second for up to 37.5 seconds. Slurp Juice can boost both Health and Shield. Once the

A refreshing gulp of Slurp Juice is a quick way to boost a soldier's Health and Shield meters.

soldier's Health reaches seventy-five, any additional points boost the soldier's Shield.

Chug Jug

A Chug Jug is an extremely powerful consumable that is rated as Legendary. It is very rare and difficult to find. Chug Jugs replenish a soldier's Health and Shield meter to one hundred. The drawback of Chug Jugs, other than their rarity,

Though difficult to find, Chug Jugs are the ultimate cure for depleted Health or Shield meters.

is that they take fifteen seconds to use, which can leave a soldier vulnerable to attack.

Bush

The Bush is a consumable that disguises a player as…a bush! It offers a great option for players who need to hide quickly to avoid detection by enemies. The drawbacks of the Bush are that a player must be completely still to use it successfully, and, if any damage whatsoever is sustained, the Bush immediately disappears.

TIPS FOR MAKING THE MOST OF THE BUSH CONSUMABLE

The Bush is a great consumable to use to hide or to ambush an opponent. There are a few things to keep in mind when using the Bush for disguise. First, remember to use the Bush disguise outdoors only, or opponents will be suspicious. There are many types of bushes on the island, so players using the Bush should position themselves near the same types of bushes. Though it seems obvious, some players forget to stay absolutely still when disguised as the Bush. To remain completely covered by the disguise, players need to crouch, rather than stand. Lastly, remember that any type of damage will extinguish the Bush disguise, so players should take care to avoid the Storm border while using this consumable.

Fortnite is a worldwide phenomenon among gamers. It offers players a fun, challenging storyline, lots of action, the ability to customize,

Fortnite is even more fun when played with friends!

and the opportunity to play as a team. For many players, the teamwork involved is a big part of what makes *Fortnite* so much fun, especially when wearing gaming headsets to talk with teammates during the game. It's important to stay safe when playing any online game, so players should end any communication with a teammate who is disrespectful or who asks personal questions or makes any comment that makes another player uncomfortable. Under those circumstances, it's always the right thing to do to end the match and take a break for a bit. However, teaming up with friends in *Fortnite*: Battle Royale can help ensure that a match will be both fun and safe, just as it should be! So find some good, reliable gaming friends to watch your back, and have fun on the island!

GLOSSARY

ATTRIBUTED Linked to or caused by.

CIRCUMSTANCES Set of conditions or factors.

CONVENIENT When something falls into place or can be accomplished with very little effort.

CROUCH A position in which the knees are bent and the person is stooping down rather than standing up.

DEPLETED Used up, drained, or spent.

DETECTION The process in which someone or something hidden is found.

DISGUISE Something worn to hide oneself or change one's appearance.

DRAWBACK A limitation or negative aspect or side effect of something.

ELIMINATED Removed or gotten rid of.

ESSENTIAL Necessary or required.

EXTINGUISH To cancel or put an end to something.

MODE A certain methodology, system, or style of something.

OPPONENTS People competing against others for something.

PERTAIN To relate to or be about something.

PHENOMENON Something very remarkable and almost unbelievable.

PHYSICIST A scientist who specializes in matter and energy.

REPLENISH To restock or fill something up again.

RESOURCES A supply of materials or money needed to be successful.

ROUTE A path or course to take to get somewhere.

SUSTAINED Suffered something or underwent something.

VALUABLE Worth a lot.

VULNERABLE In a dangerous, unprotected situation.

FOR MORE INFORMATION

Entertainment Software Association of Canada
Website: http://theesa.ca

Enthusiast Gaming
Website: http://www.enthusiastgaming.com

Epic Games
Website: https://www.epicgames.com/fortnite/en-US/home

ESports Foundation, Inc.
Website: https://esports.us

FOR FURTHER READING

Bossom, Andy, and Ben Dunning. *Video Games: An Introduction to the Industry*. New York, NY: Fairchild Books, 2016.

Kuhn, Damien. *The* Fortnite *Guide to Staying Alive*. Kansas City, MO: Andrews McMeel Publishing, 2018.

Li, Roland. *Good Luck Have Fun: The Rise of eSports*. New York, NY: Skyhorse Publishing, 2016.

Rich, Jason R. *An Encyclopedia of Strategy for* Fortniters*: An Unofficial Guide for Battle Royale*. New York, NY: Sky Pony Press, 2018.

Rich, Jason R. Fortnite Battle Royale *Hacks: Advanced Strategies*. New York, NY: Sky Pony Press, 2018.

Rich, Jason R. *Ultimate Unofficial Survival Tactics for* Fortnite Battle Royale*: Mastering Game Settings for Victory*. New York, NY: Sky Pony Press, 2019.

Shofner, Melissa. *Video Game Developer*. New York, NY: Rosen Publishing, 2018.

Taylor, T. L. *Watch Me Play: Twitch and the Rise of Game Live Streaming*. Princeton, NJ: Princeton University Press, 2018.

Triumph Books. *The Big Book of* Fortnite*: The Deluxe Unofficial Guide to Battle Royale*. Chicago, IL: Triumph Books, 2018.

Triumph Books. Fortnite*: The Essential Guide to Battle Royale and Other Survival Games*. Chicago, IL: Triumph Books, 2018.

INDEX

About the Author

Jessica Shaw holds a BA in psychology from Texas State University. She has worked in human services and as a preschool teacher. She writes nonfiction, fiction, and poetry for children and young adults, including standardized testing material and work appearing in numerous children's publications.

Photo Credits

Cover Fuse/Corbis/Getty Images; p. 5 Brookhaven National Laboratory/Wikimedia Commons/File:50th Anniversary Tennis For Two.jpg/PD; p. 9 Ethan Miller/Getty Images; p. 14 Rokas Tenys/Shutterstock.com; p. 22 Veja/Shutterstock.com; p. 25 wundervisuals/iStock/Getty Images Plus/Getty Images.

Design & Layout: Brian Garvey
Editor: Bethany Bryan
Photo Researcher: Nicole DiMella
Fortnite Consultant: Sam Keppeler